Holly Wright

Charles Wright
SESTETS

Charles Wright, winner of the Pulitzer Prize, the
National Book Critics Circle Award, the National
Book Award, and the Griffin Poetry Prize, teaches at
the University of Virginia in Charlottesville.

ALSO BY CHARLES WRIGHT

POETRY

The Grave of the Right Hand
Hard Freight
Bloodlines
China Trace
The Southern Cross
Country Music: Selected Early Poems
The Other Side of the River
Zone Journals
Xionia
The World of the Ten Thousand Things: Poems 1980–1990
Chickamauga
Black Zodiac
Appalachia
North American Bear
Negative Blue: Selected Later Poems
A Short History of the Shadow
Buffalo Yoga
Scar Tissue
Littlefoot

TRANSLATIONS

The Storm and Other Things (Eugenio Montale)
Orphic Songs (Dino Campana)

NONFICTION

Halflife
Quarter Notes

SESTETS

SESTETS

CHARLES WRIGHT

FARRAR, STRAUS AND GIROUX   NEW YORK

Farrar, Straus and Giroux
18 West 18th Street, New York 10011

Copyright © 2009 by Charles Wright
All rights reserved

Printed in the United States of America
Published in 2009 by Farrar, Straus and Giroux
First paperback edition, 2010

Grateful acknowledgment is made to the following magazines, in whose pages some of these poems first appeared: *Appalachian Anthology*, *The Believer*, *Blackbird*, *The Fiddlehead* (Canada), *FIELD*, *Harvard Divinity Bulletin*, *The Massachussetts Review*, *The New Republic*, *The New Yorker*, *The New York Review of Books*, *Northwest Review*, *The Paris Review*, *The Southern Quarterly*, *Tight*, *Tin House*, *Venti Quattro*, and *Virginia Quarterly Review*.

The Library of Congress has cataloged the hardcover edition as follows:
Wright, Charles, 1935–
    Sestets / Charles Wright.— 1st ed.
        p.   cm.
    ISBN: 978-0-374-26115-3 (alk. paper)
    I. Title.

PS3573.R52S47 2009
811'.54—dc22

2008033990

Paperback ISBN: 978-0-374-53214-7

Designed by Jonathan D. Lippincott

www.fsgbooks.com

For Luke, who is the Doctor

Contents

SESTETS

Tomorrow

The metaphysics of the quotidian was what he was after:
A little dew on the sunrise grass,
A drop of blood in the evening trees,

                              a drop of fire.

If you don't shine you are darkness.
The future is merciless,

                    everyone's name inscribed
On the flyleaf of the Book of Snow.

The Gospel According to Somebody Else

Comfort them all, Lord, comfort their odd shapes

and their standard hair.

They seem so hand-haunted, so hymn-hewn,

In their slow drift toward received form.

Comfort them standing there,

then comfort them sitting down—

God knows his own, the old have no tears,

The thickness of winter clouds is the thickness of what's to come.

Future Tense

All things in the end are bittersweet—
An empty gaze, a little way station just beyond silence.

If you can't delight in the everyday,
                                        you have no future here.
And if you can, no future either.

And time, black dog, will sniff you out,
                                        and lick your lean cheeks,
And lie down beside you—warm, real close—and will not move.

Flannery's Angel

Lead us to those we are waiting for,
Those who are waiting for us.
May your wings protect us,
                may we not be strangers in the lush province of joy.

Remember us who are weak,
You who are strong in your country which lies beyond the thunder,
Raphael, angel of happy meeting,
                      resplendent, hawk of the light.

Cowboy Up

There comes a time in one's life when one wants time,
                              a lot of time, with inanimate things.
Not ultimate inanimate things,
Of course, but mute things,
                              beautiful, untalkbackable wise things.
That's wishful thinking, cowboy.

Still, I'd like to see the river of stars
                  fall noiselessly through the nine heavens for once,
But the world's weight, and the world's welter, speak big talk and
    big confusion.

In Praise of What Is Missing

When a tooth is extracted,
              some side of the holy wheel is unnotched,
And twists, unlike Ixion's, in the wind and weather,
And one slips into wanting nothing more
                               from the human world,
And leans back, a drifting cloud,
Toward what becomes vacant and is nameless and is blue,
As days once were, and will be again.

By the Waters of Babylon

We live on Orphan Mountain,
                    each of us, and that's how it is,
Kingfisher still wet
And chattering on his empty branch.

Water remains immortal—
Poems can't defile it,
                    the heron, immobile on one leg,
Stands in it, snipe stitch it, and heaven pillows its breast.

Hasta la Vista Buckaroo

So many have come and gone, undone
                              like a rhinestone cowboy,
Dazzle and snuff, Lord, dazzle and snuff,
In a two-bit rodeo.

The entrance to hell is just a tiny hole in the ground,
The size of an old pecan, soul-sized, horizon-sized.
Thousands go through it each day before the mist clears
                              thousands one by one you're next.

Double Salt

1.

The crystal body of wind,

                    deep blue and *macchiato* by one cloud

Over White Hall, light like a river

Flooding the underweave,

                        azaleas pink and white in the 10th heaven,

As Dante would note,

Fingerlings of the maple chartreuse

                            against the radiance of the nine-ply

Answer to everything down the corridor we have to walk . . .

2.

Virgo halfway across the heavens when

the sun goes down,

Late August, cicadas in medias res, eighth
Moon, and no one the wiser.

No matter what anyone says,

life and death are not equal—

No matter what time of year,
No matter how loud the grasshopper sings,

no matter how far he flies.

Born Again II

Take me down to the river,
                    the ugly, reseasoned river.
Add on me a sin or two,
Then cleanse me, and wash me, O white-shirted Pardoner.

Suerte, old friend.
The caravan's come and gone, the dogs have stopped barking,
And nothing remains but the sound of the water monotonous,
                                              and the wind.

No Entry

It is not possible to imagine and feel the pain of others.
We say we do but we don't.
It is a country we have no passport for,

and no right of entry.

Empathy is emphatic,

and sends long lines across the floor.
But it's not the hurt or wound.
It's not the secret of the black raven,

cut out by water into oblivion.

Celestial Waters

May 30th, early evening,
                     one duck on the narrow water, pond
Stocked with clouds,
The world reflected and windless, full of grace, tiny, tiny.

Osiris has shown us the way to cross the coming night sky,
The route, the currents, the necessary magic words.
Stick to your business, boys,
                     and forget the down-below.

Anniversary II

Dun-colored moth past the windowpane.

                                 Now, he's got the right idea,

Fuzzy and herky-jerky,

                little Manichaean

Pulled by invisible strings toward light wherever it is.

On the 5th of June, the mother is like a shining,

Blue raindrop the sunlight refracts

                             on the tip of the spruce tree,

Crack in the bulbous sky the moth is yo-yoed up to.

Outscape

There's no way to describe how the light splays
                                 after the storm, under the clouds
Still piled like Armageddon
Back to the west, the northwest,
                      intent on incursion.

There's no way to picture it,
                 though others have often tried to.
Here in the mountains it's like a ricochet from a sea surge,
Meadow grass moving like sea stalks
                     in the depths of its brilliance.

Sunlight Bets on the Come

The basic pleasures remain unchanged,
                              and their minor satisfactions—
Chopping wood, building a fire,
Watching the elk herd
          splinter and cruise around the outcrop of spruce trees

As the deer haul ass,
                    their white flags like synchronized swimmers' hands,
Sunlight sealing—stretched like Saran Wrap—
The world as we know it,
                    keeping it fresh-flamed should tomorrow arrive.

"Well, Get Up, Rounder,
Let a Working Man Lay Down"

The kingdom of minutiae,
                    that tight place where most of us live,
Is the kingdom of the saved,
Those who exist between the cracks,
                                those just under the details.

When the hand comes down, the wing-white hand,
We are the heads of hair
                    and finger bones yanked out of their shoes,
We are the Rapture's children.

Consolation and the Order of the World

There is a certain hubris,
                            or sense of invulnerability,
That sends us packing
Whenever our focus drops a stop, or the flash fails.

These snaps are the balance of our lives,
Defining moments, permanent signs,
Fir shadows needling out of the woods,
                            night with its full syringe.

Return of the Prodigal

Now comes summer, water clear, clouds heavy with weeping.
Tall grasses are silver-veined.
Little puddles of sunlight collect
                    in low places deep in the woods.

Lupine and paintbrush stoic in ditch weed,
                 larch rust a smear on the mountainside.
No light on ridgeline.
Zodiac pinwheels across the heavens,
                  bat-feint under Gemini.

With Horace, Sitting on the Platform,
Waiting for the Robert E. Lee

Seventy years, and what's left?

                     Or better still, what's gone before?

A couple of lines, a day or two out in the cold?

And all those books, those half-baked books,

                       sweet yeast for the yellow dust?

What say, Orazio? Like you, I'm sane and live at the edge of things,

Countryside flooded with light,

Sundown,

     the chaos of future mornings just over the ridge, but not here yet.

The Song from the Other Side of the World

We haven't heard from the void lately.

Such a wonderful spot,

There's coffee and bananas and the temperature's hot.

So lush a voice, so lambent a tune.

Must be a bad frequency.

Our astral music, however, will come back, and harbor us

As we go gliding, lashed to the mast,

into its sensual waters.

The Gospel According to Yours Truly

Tell me again, Lord, how easy it all is—

renounce this,

Renounce that, and all is a shining—
Tell me again, I'm still here,

your quick-lipped and malleable boy.

(Strange how the clouds bump and grind, and the underthings roll,
Strange how the grasses finger and fondle each other—
I renounce them, I renounce them, I renounce them.

Gnarly and thin, the nothings don't change . . .)

The Evening Is Tranquil,
and Dawn Is a Thousand Miles Away

The mares go down for their evening feed
                                        into the meadow grass.
Two pine trees sway the invisible wind—
                                        some sway, some don't sway.
The heart of the world lies open, leached and ticking with sunlight
For just a minute or so.
The mares have their heads on the ground,
                        the trees have their heads on the blue sky.
Two ravens circle and twist.
            On the borders of heaven, the river flows clear a bit longer.

Homage to What's-His-Name

Ah, description, of all the arts the least appreciated.
Well, it's just this and it's just that,
                                    someone will point out.
Exactly. It's just this and it's just that and nothing other.

From landscape to unsuppressed conjunction, it's only itself.
No missteps, no misreading.
                            And what's more metaphysical than that,
The world in its proper posture, on all fours, drinking the sweet water?

Tutti Frutti

"A-wop-bop-a-loo-lop a-lop-bam-boo,"

                    Little Richard in full gear—
What could be better than that?
Not much that I know of, at least not in my green time.

It's hard, O, my, it is hard,
To find a sustainable ecstasy, and make it endure.
Detail, detail, detail—God and the Devil
                    hang side by side between each break.

"This World Is Not My Home,
I'm Only Passing Through"

The more you say, the more mistakes you'll make,

                                                 so keep it simple.

No one arrives without leaving soon.

This blue-eyed, green-footed world—

                                   hello, Goldie, goodbye.

We won't meet again. So what?

The rust will remain in the trees,

                                and pine needles stretch their necks,

Their tiny necks, and sunlight will snore in the limp grass.

Stiletto

Why does each evening up here
                always, in summer, seem to be
The way—as it does, with the light knifing low from right to left—
It will be on the next-to-last one?

The next-to-last one for me, I mean.
There is no music involved,
                so it must be the light, and its bright blade.
The last one, of course, will be dark.
                And the knife will be dark too.

"*I Shall Be Released*"

There is a consolation beyond nomenclature
                                        of what is past
Or is about to pass, though I don't know what it is.
But someone, somewhere, must, and this is addressed to him.

Come on, Long Eyes, crack the book.
Thumb through the pages and stop at the one with the golden script.
Breathe deeply and lay it on me,
                        that character with the luminous half-life.

Description's the Art of Something or Other

Description is expiation,
                                and not a place to hunker down in.
It is a virtual world
Unfit for the virtuous.
                                It is a coming to terms with.

Or coming to terms without.
As though whatever we had to say could keep it real.
As though our words were flies,
                                and the dead meat kept reappearing.

"It's Sweet to Be Remembered"

No one's remembered much longer than a rock
                              is remembered beside the road
If he's lucky or
Some tune or harsh word
                    uttered in childhood or back in the day.

Still how nice to imagine some kid someday
                    picking that rock up and holding it in his hand
Briefly before he chucks it
Deep in the woods in a sunny spot in the tall grass.

Basin Creek Sundown

And the air remains timeless over the ridge back, and the clouds
Tangled in light and the pentimento of blue sky,
Trees swaying to unknown music
                              that only they hear.

Nothing else matters, Henri, but this,
The movement of all things, come and go
Of all things,
                 the whisper of dusk in the drowsy ear.

In Memory of the Natural World

Four ducks on the pond tonight, the fifth one MIA.
A fly, a smaller than normal fly,
Is mapping his way through sun-strikes across my window.

Behind him, as though at attention,
                                the pine trees hold their breaths.
The fly's real, the trees are real,
And the ducks.
                But the glass is artificial, and it's on fire.

Yellow Wings

When the sun goes down—and you happen to notice it—
And the sky is clear, there's always a whitish light
                              edging the earth's offerings.
This is the lost, impermanent light
The soul is pulled toward, and longs for, deep in its cave,
Little canary.
This is the light its wings dissolve in
                      if it ever gets out from underground.

Twilight of the Dogs

Death is the mother of nothing.
                              This is a fact of life,
And exponentially sad.
All these years—a lifetime, really—thinking it might be otherwise.

What are the colors of despair?
                              Are they calibrated, like vowels?
How will we know them?
Who knows where the light will fall
                              as the clouds go from west to the east?

Remembering Bergamo Alto

A postapocalyptic poetry
                    starts with a dog bite
And featherless birds in the ruined trees,
People nowhere to be found.

Mostly it has to do with cities,
                    and empty boulevards,
Chairs in the public parks with no one to sit in them.
Mostly it's wind in vacant spaces,
                    and piano chords from a high window.

With Alighieri on Basin Creek

All four of the ducks are gone now.

        Only the mountain remains,
Upside down like Purgatorio
In the pond's reflection,

      no tree at the top, and no rivers.

No matter. Above it, in either incarnation,
The heavens, in all their golden numbers, begin to unstack.
Down here, as night comes on, we look for Guido,
  his once best friend, and Guido's father, and Bertran de Born.

Walking Beside the Diversion Ditch Lake

I love to make the kingfishers fly
                    from their bony perches
Above the lake, six or seven, one after the next,
Circling the water and chattering back,
                    as I walk along.

Can the fish hear them?
Is their cry like organ chording,
                    leading to one vast ultimate stop?
Who was it who first said, "The kingfisher falls through fire"?

Next

The Great Scribe, who remembers nothing,
              not even your name the instant he writes it down,
Would like it up here, I think,
The blank page of the sundown sky, the tamarack quill points,
                    and no one to answer for.

This would be a tough story to crack.
Who wouldn't embrace such an absence,
Especially someone whose page is always full,
                  and whose narrative goes nowhere?

The Ghost of Walter Benjamin Walks at Midnight

The world's an untranslatable language
                                        without words or parts of speech.
It's a language of objects
Our tongues can't master,
                                but which we are the ardent subjects of.

If *tree* is *tree* in English,
                                and *albero* in Italian,
That's as close as we can come
To divinity, the language that circles the earth
                                        and which we'll never speak.

Bees Are the Terrace Builders of the Stars

It's odd how the objects of our lives
Continue to not define us,

                no matter how close we hold them unto us.
Odd how the narrative of those lives is someone else's narrative.

Now the increasing sundown.

                The Bible draws the darkness around it,
No footbridge or boat over Lethe,
No staircase or stepping-stone

                up into the Into.

Timetable

It is the hour of transmutation.
The great blue heron flaps up the creek
                           like a skeletal, excommunicated nun.
Similes sift through my hands.

Bone-dusted coffins drift downriver.
The smell of something store-sweet comes in through the open
    window.
Darkness, the great enveloper, envelops nothing.

When the Horses Gallop Away from Us,
It's a Good Thing

I always find it strange—though I shouldn't—how creatures don't
    care for us the way we care for them.
Horses, for instance, and chipmunks, and any bird you'd name.
Empathy's only a one-way street.

And that's all right, I've come to believe.
It sets us up for ultimate things,
                        and penultimate ones as well.
It's a good lesson to have in your pocket when the Call comes to
    call.

Autumn Is Visionary, Summer's the Same Old Stuff

Half-moon rising, thin as a contact lens.

                           The sun going down
As effortlessly as a body through deep water,
Both at the same time, simple pleasures
As autumn begins to rustle and rinse,

                           as autumn begins to prink.

And now the clouds come on,

                        the same clouds that Turner saw.
Half of the moon sees them, half does not.

Bitter Herbs to Eat, and Dipped in Honey

We lay out our own dark end,

                              guilt, and the happiness of guilt.

God never enters into it, nor

Do his pale hands and pale wings,

                              angel of time he has become.

The wind doesn't blow in the soul,

                              so no boat there for passage.

Half paths of the half-moon, then,

To walk up and down in the forest,

                              to walk hard in the bright places.

No Angel

In the Kingdom of the Hollow-at-Heart, the insect is king.
In the Kingdom of the Beyond,
                      all lie where the ground is smooth.
Everything's what it seems to be, and a little less.

In the land of the unutterable,
                      words float like reflections across the water.
Nobody visits us here.
Like shadows, we spread ourselves until our hands touch,
                          then disappear in the dark.

Basin Creek Lullaby

Awake, this is all an illusion, they say.
                                    Asleep, it's a repeat,
I hasten to add, the same odd taste of bitterness
And terror, the same sensation
                          of falling, no it's flying, no, it's falling.

Grasshoppers assuage us, deer wheeze through the downed timber.
At least we think they do so.
A pair of sparrow hawks goes from tree to tree.
              They're not in the grasshopper's dream. Nor ours.

Time Is a Graceless Enemy,
but Purls as It Comes and Goes

I'm winding down. The daylight is winding down.
                              Only the night is wound up tight,
And ticking with unpaused breath.
Sweet night, sweet steady, reliable, uncomplicated night.

September moon, two days from full,
                              slots up from the shouldered hill.
There is no sound as the moon slots up, no thorns in its body.
Invisible, the black gondola floats
                              through down-lid and drowning stars.

49

The Great Blue Heron and the Tree of Night

Great blue on a dead limb, high up in the tree, air fishing,
Legs stiff and straight as though in water,
Huge head and cyclotron eyes
                    focusing on the deep, slow currents of evening,
Waiting for anything to come close.

Try to imagine him standing there for all eternity,
Sun going down, sun coming up, and no gain.
                                    What would he care?

Terrestrial Music

What's up, grand architect of the universe?
                                    The stars are falling,
The moon is failing behind your vaporous laundry,
Planets are losing their names,
                and darkness is dropping inches beneath the earth.

Down here, we take it in stride.
The horses go on with their chomp and snatch in the long grasses,
The dogs cringe,
               and coyotes sing in the still woods, back out of sight.

Before the Propane Lamps Come On,
the World Is a Risk and Wonder

Sundown smoke like a pink snood
                    over the gathered hair of the mountains,
The sun a garish hatpin
Incongruous in the netting and underfold of the day.

The creek's voice is constant,
                    and like a shadow embraces many things.
I wish it were my voice, but it's not.
My voice is a human thing, and weak,
                    and it disappears with the sun.

Autumn Thoughts on the East Fork

Daytime is boredom after a while, I've come to find, and
    nighttime too.
But in between,
    when the evening starts to drain the seen world into the unseen,
And the mare's-tail clouds swish slowly across the mountains,

Contentment embraces me
With its spidery arms and its spade-tipped, engendering tail.
There must be a Chinese character for this, a simple one,
                     but we've never seen it up here.

Little Meditation Above the Meadow

The beautiful brown of the autumn grasses—
                              now upright after a strong wind—
Is like the green of the evergreens,
Awkwardly upward, but cinching the earth to the sky.

Our poor lives would like that color—
                              actually, either one of them—
To turn us into an otherwise,
Something that mindlessly displays,
                              something that connects.

On the Night of the First Snow,
Thinking About Tennessee

It's dark now, the horses have had their half apple,
                                              mist and rain,
Horses down in the meadow, just a few degrees above snow.

I stand in front of the propane stove, warming my legs.

If the door were open, I'd listen to creek water
And think I heard voices from long ago,
                              distinct, and calling me home.

The past becomes such a mirror—we're in it, and then we're not.

Our Days Are Political, but Birds Are Something Else

Tenth month of the year.
                    Fallen leaves taste bitter. And grass.
Everything that we've known, and come to count on,
                                        has fled the world.
Their bones crack in the west wind.

Where are the deeds we're taught to cling to?
How I regret having missed them,
                        and their mirrored pieces of heaven.
Like egrets, they rise in the clear sky,
                    their shadows like distance on the firred hills.

We Hope That Love Calls Us,
but Sometimes We're Not So Sure

No wind-sighs. And rain-splatter heaves up over the mountains,
                                                    and dies out.
October humidity
Like a heart-red tower light,
                        now bright, now not so bright.

Autumn night at the end of the world.
In its innermost corridors,
                        all damp and all light are gone, and love, too.
Amber does not remember the pine.

Only the I-Ching Hexagrams Are Lacking

Unlike despair, happiness knows no final answer.
As one who has carried discontent
Like car keys,
            why should I silence the music of their ping and jingle?

I turn to the Master of No Speech
And seek his counsel.
            In the dye-glare of Zattere waters,
He opens his hands: five elements and the ten celestial stems.

Time Is a Dark Clock,
but It Still Strikes from Time to Time

Whump-di-ump-whump-whump,

                          tweedilee tweedilee tweedilidee,

I'm as happy as can be . . .

Pretty nice, but that was then,

                  when our hearts were meat on the grill.

And who was it, Etta James or Ruth Brown or LaVern Baker?

The past is so dark, you need a flashlight to find your own shoes.

But what shoes! and always half an inch off the floor,

                  your feet like wind inside them.

Like the New Moon,
My Mother Drifts Through the Night Sky

Beyond the boundaries of light and dark,
                    my mother's gone out and not come back.
Suddenly now, in my backyard, like the slip moon she rises
And rests in my watching eye.

In my dreams she's returned just like this, over a hundred times.
She knows what I'm looking for,
Partially her,
                    partially what she comes back not to tell me.

As the Train Rolls Through, I Remember an Old Poem

Well, here we are again, old friend, Ancient of Days,
Eyeball to eyeball.
I blink, of course,
                    I blink more than ten thousand times.

Dear ghost, I picture you thus, eventually like
St. Francis in his hair shirt,
                    naked, walking the winter woods,
Singing his own song in the tongue of the troubadours.

April Evening

Spring buzz-cut on the privet hedge,

                             a couple of yellow cups

Downdrafting from the honeysuckle.

One bird in the hapless holly tree,

                             giving us liftoff and glide.

It is amazing how beautiful springtime can be,

Bell jar over our ills and endless infirmities,

Transparancy into where we know

                             the light will never reach us.

As a Pine Tree by the Waters

It's odd how the incandescent pine trees reenact
The Passion,
           or the passion, say, after the Passion, because
We live in a post-Passionate world,
Still here,
           but dead branches from the roots.
The green on top bewilders the late-evening sunlight.
Trees die from the top down;
                     we die from the bottom up.

The Book

Whose name will be inscribed in the book
                                    just before mine?
From what country, from what unburiable ever?
Somebody I'll never know, for sure,
Somebody whose fingers will never outline my face.

A splinter of his death will always remain in mine,
However,
            no matter how thick, no matter how thin.

Sundown Blues

There are some things that can't be conveyed—
                                        description, for instance,
The sundown light on that dog-hair lodgepole pine
                        and the dead branches of spruce trees.

They hold its brilliance close against them
For a tick or two
                        before it chameleons away.
No one is able to describe this gold to bronze to charcoal, no one.
So move along, boy, just move along.

"On the Trail of the Lonesome Pine"

The older I become, the more the landscape resembles me.
All morning a misty rain,
All afternoon the sun uncovered and covered by cloud snares.

At night, in the evergreens,
The moonlight slides off the wind-weary branches, and will not stick.
No movement, the dark forest.

Music for Midsummer's Eve

Longest day of the year, but still, I'd say,

                                     too short by half.

The horses whacked, the dog gone lost in the mucked, long grass,

Tree shadows crawling toward their dark brothers across the field.

Time is an untuned harmonium

That Muzaks our nights and days.

Sometimes it lasts for a little while,

                                sometimes it goes on forever.

No Direction Home

After a certain age, there's no one left to turn to.
You've got to find Eurydice on your own,
                              you've got
To find the small crack
            between here and everywhere else all by yourself.

How could it be otherwise?
Everyone's gone away, the houses are all empty,
And overcast starts to fill the sky like soiled insulation.

Hovercraft

Hummingbird stopped as a period, breast embossed

                                  purple-pink-crimson

Outside the northside window,

Wings invisible in their stillness,

                         unquiet, never faltering.

And then, whoosh, he's gone,

Leaving a little hole in the air, one that the air

                                  doesn't rush in to fill.

Empty pocket.

           The world, and the other world, are full of them.

Time Is a Child-Biting Dog

Like rivers, my thoughts flow south,

                  for no particular reason.

Must be the full moon

That floods the sky, and makes the night wakeful

                  and full of remorse.

It's not here yet, but give it an hour or so, then we,

Bewildered, who want our poems to be clouds

                  upholding the sour light of heaven,

Will pass our gray hair through our fingers

                  and sigh just a little bit.

Nothing Is Written

In a couple of hours, it will start all over again,
The stars will lean down and stare from their faceless spaces,
And the moon will boot up on the black screen of the sky,
                              humping toward God-knows-what,

And we, with our pinched mouths and pinched eyes, the next
        morning
Will see its footprint like a slice of snow
                              torn off over Caribou,
Looking for somewhere else to be born.

Little Ending

Bowls will receive us,
                 and sprinkle black scratch in our eyes.
Later, at the great fork on the untouchable road,
It won't matter where we have become.

Unburdened by prayer, unburdened by any supplication,
Someone will take our hand,
                 someone will give us refuge,
Circling left or circling right.

NOTES

"Celestial Waters": Roberto Calasso, *K.*, translated by Geoffrey Brock, chapter VI, Vintage Books, 2005.

"Return of the Prodigal": Template of something vaguely remembered I'd read in Pound some forty years ago, a Chinese calendar. Actually about the return of my son from England, June 2006, after twelve years abroad. Second day of summer, June 22, also involved.

"Homage to What's-His-Name" is for Mark Strand.

"Hovercraft": John McIntire, June 27, 1907.

9 780374 532147